FLAGS
OF
AMERICAN
HISTORY

FLAGS OF

by
DAVID D. CROUTHERS
Formerly Map Librarian
C. S. Hammond & Company

Flag Illustrations by
NICHOLAS ZARRELLI

AMERICAN HISTORY

C. S. Hammond & Company

Maplewood, New Jersey

Contents

Checklist of Flags

☆ 9

The Pledge of Allegiance

I pledge allegiance
to the Flag
of the
United States of America
and to the Republic
for which it stands,
one Nation under God,
indivisible,
with liberty and justice
for all.

(U. S. CODE, 1958 ED., SEC. 172)

Note to the Reader

"Flags of American History" describes briefly and portrays, in full color, a comprehensive selection of the flags which have played a living part in American history from the beginnings of European settlement on these shores to the present day. Most of the familiar banners have been included, together with a variety of flags of obscure background or unusual history.

Many of these flags flew proudly for many years as the emblems of mighty nations. Indeed, several of them still do; others fluttered in brief glory during a bloody battle or grim siege. All of them have, in one fashion or another, embodied the hopes and emotions of those who struggled in bitter combat or prospered in happy peace beneath them.

Any extended study about our flag eventually calls into question the customs, etiquette, or traditions pertaining to this national symbol. It is often difficult to locate material supplying adequate information. This volume attempts, in so far as space permits, to present authoritative answers and to indicate the points at which fact and historical legend have become intertwined.

The flags are arranged to provide easy reference with the annotations as concise as is consistent with clarity. *Italics* refer to the flags illustrated. At the time of their use, some of them were not known by a specific name. The checklist of state flags furnishes identification of each of the fifty state banners.

It is hoped that the reader will gain accurate knowledge of each flag herein, both visually and through the text. Librarians and teachers have suggested that the section on Flag Etiquette be presented in the same form in which it appears in the U.S. Code of Laws. This assures the reader that the text is official and that all amendments have been included.

It is interesting to note that where the word "Don't" is used on early American flags, it appears without an apostrophe. Examples of this are "Dont Tread on Me" on the Rattlesnake Flag and "Dont Give Up the Ship" on Commodore Perry's Flag.

The Americans Creed

I believe in the United States of America as a Government of the people, by the people, for the people; whose just powers are derived from the consent of the governed; a democracy in a republic; a sovereign Nation of many sovereign States; a perfect union, one and inseparable; established upon those principles of freedom, equality, justice and humanity for which American patriots sacrificed their lives and fortunes.

I therefore believe it is my duty to my country to love it; to support its Constitution; to obey its laws; to respect its flag, and to defend it against all enemies.

THIS CREED WAS WRITTEN IN 1917 BY WILLIAM TYLER PAGE. IT WAS ACCEPTED FOR THE AMERICAN PEOPLE, BY THE HOUSE OF REPRESENTATIVES, ON APRIL 3, 1918.

FLAGS
OF
AMERICAN
HISTORY

Colonial Flags   1

Flags have been an important element in American history since the first days of European exploration and settlement on the American continent. During the sixteenth and seventeenth centuries flags symbolized the rivalry and ambitions of competing and expanding nations. However, our story begins earlier, about the year 1000, when Eric the Red, Leif Ericson, and other intrepid Viking explorers made wide-ranging voyages of exploration from their Scandinavian homeland. These Norse adventurers flew, according to tradition, the *Viking Banner* of Scandinavia on their journeys to Iceland, Greenland and, presumably, North America. On this banner the black raven, a familiar favorite to the Norsemen, appears on a white field.

VIKING BANNER

COLUMBUS' STANDARD

European interest in the western continent was, however, aimless and indefinite until the momentous trip of Christopher Columbus at the end of the fifteenth century. Columbus sailed on his voyages of exploration and discovery to the West Indies and South America under the flag of Ferdinand and Isabella, joint sovereigns of the newly united Kingdom of Spain. This Spanish flag, *Columbus' Standard,* is the emblem which he planted on San Salvador (Watling's Island) in the Bahamas on October 12, 1492. But, in addition to the Spanish colors, Columbus had a personal pennant bearing the Cross and the initials

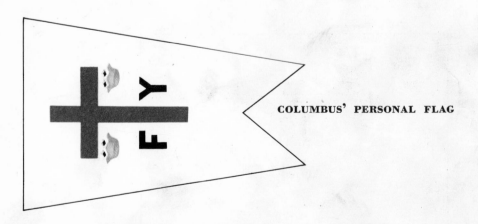

COLUMBUS' PERSONAL FLAG

of his patrons, Ferdinand and Isabella. It is designated here as *Columbus' Personal Flag.*

Soon after Spain arrived on the American scene, other European powers began to show interest in the new continent. Explorers in the service of England began to appear along North American coasts a few years after Columbus' first voyage. The red *Cross of St. George,* for centuries the national flag of England, was flown by John and Sebastian Cabot on their voyages of discovery to Newfoundland and the North American continent in 1497; as well as by other early English explorers and voyagers to North America, including Sir Walter Raleigh and Sir Humphrey Gilbert.

**CROSS OF
ST. GEORGE**

**CROSS OF
ST. ANDREW**

St. Andrew's Cross, strictly speaking, in the language of heraldry, a saltire rather than a cross, was used in early Scottish attempts at settlement in Nova Scotia. It was joined in 1603 with St. George's Cross to form the famous Union Flag or "Union Jack" of Great Britain which flew over the British colonies in North America for more than a century and a half.

New Sweden, a small Swedish colony on the lower Delaware River, flew the blue and yellow *Flag of Sweden,* essentially the same as the Swedish flag of today, from 1638 until 1655 when the settlement was annexed to New Amsterdam by the Dutch.

The *Dutch East India Company,* for which Henry Hudson sailed, and the *Dutch West India Company,* which was responsible for the settlement of New Amsterdam, both used as flags variations of the well-known tricolor flag of the Netherlands. The flags differ in the color of the upper stripe because the original orange color, used in honor of the House of Orange, was changed during this period to red

DUTCH EAST
INDIA COMPANY
FLAG

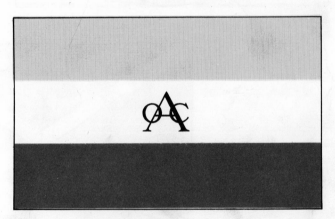

in order to insure better visibility during inclement weather. The initials A.O.C. and G.W.C. indicate in the Dutch language, respectively, the Dutch East India Company and the Dutch West India Company.

Of greater importance than the settlements of the Swedes and the Dutch were the more elaborate and prolonged ventures of the French. The famous *Lily Banner,* in use in various forms since the Middle Ages, was the flag of widespread French exploration and settlement in North

22 ☆

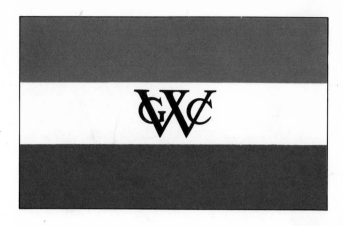

America from Quebec and the Great Lakes to Louisiana and the West Indies. The explorers Joliet, Marquette, La Salle, Iberville, and Bienville, all traveled under this flag. France had still another flag, a plain white one, the *Bourbon Banner*. It was under this flag that Champlain conducted his explorations. This snow-white flag of the Bourbons was also flown at a much later time by the French naval forces which came in 1781 to the aid of the rebelling American colonists.

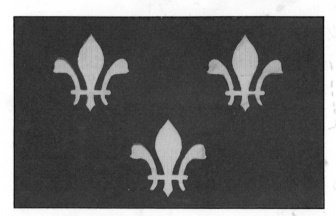

LILY BANNER

BOURBON BANNER

ENDICOTT FLAG

THREE COUNTY TROOP STANDARD

The flags of Spain, Sweden, the Netherlands, and France played prominent roles during the history of pre-Revolutionary America. Nevertheless, it was the flags of British origin, or at least British associations, which were most frequently encountered during the seventeenth and eighteenth centuries. Many of these flags were used over a limited area and, as often as not, rather informally. A great number of such local flags were current in Massachusetts as well as the other New England colonies. One early example was the *Endicott Flag*, which took its name from a colonial governor, John Endicott, of Salem, Massachusetts. Adopted in 1634, it was actually a form of the English Red Ensign.

The three Massachusetts counties of Suffolk, Middlesex and Essex joined together in 1659 to raise a troop of cavalry. This cavalry troop existed for a number of years and is believed to have taken part in King Philip's War, an important seventeenth century New England conflict. The group carried a distinctive flag generally called the *Three County Troop Standard*.

The New England colonies soon developed commercial interests along with a flourishing maritime trade. Colonial merchant vessels flew a number of different ensigns. One of these, a *Colonial Ensign,* another version of the English Red Ensign, is shown here. It became a popular and widely used flag in New England.

During their earlier years the New England colonies were really semi-independent states; but near the end of the seventeenth century the home government in London began to move toward greater centralization. In line with this policy, Sir Edmund Andros was appointed, in 1687, to be governor of the short-lived Dominion of New England, which comprised the New England colonies, New York and New Jersey. Governor Andros employed *this flag,* a version of the Cross of St. George bearing the monogram of King James II of England. In 1701 ships registered in colonial ports were required to hoist the *Union Jack with a white shield, or "escutcheon,"* in the center of the flag in order to distinguish themselves from ships registered in British ports.

ANDROS' FLAG

COLONIAL ENSIGN

ESCUTCHEONED
JACK

NEW ENGLAND
FLAG

At the same time local groups of colonists were still busily devising local flags. Here is an example, known simply as the *New England Flag*, with a blue field substituted for the traditional red, thereby causing the flag to resemble another British sea flag, the Blue Ensign.

MARYLAND STATE FLAG

UNION FLAG

Although the *Maryland State Flag* was adopted officially as recently as 1904, it had been in use since the middle of the seventeenth century as a flag distinctive of Maryland. It was in use in England long before that as the banner of the Calvert family. The design is drawn from the coat of arms of Lord Baltimore (George Calvert), the proprietor of the Maryland colony. It is a most striking and interesting flag.

The old British *Union Flag* or, more colloquially, the "Union Jack," which differs slightly from the Union Flag of today, is perhaps the most famous flag in all history. (A jack is a small flag flown at the bow of naval and, occasionally, other vessels.) It flew over the British colonies in North America from the landing of the first colonists at Jamestown in 1607, and at Plymouth in 1620, until the Revolution. It flew over what was to become United States territory longer than any other flag. Although flown as a jack by ships, the Union Flag was, and is today, used chiefly on land. When used as a military flag, it frequently bears regimental badges and is referred to as the "King's (or Queen's) Color." The Union Flag was designed in 1603 at the time of the union of the Crowns of England and Scotland and combined, ratherly cleverly, the long-established national flags of England and Scotland, the Cross of St. George, and the Cross of St. Andrew.

A number of British maritime flags, or ensigns, are formed by

RED ENSIGN

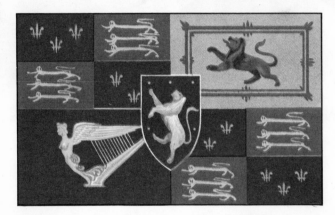

ROYAL STANDARD

placing the Union Flag in the canton (the upper corner near the staff) of another flag having a field of white, blue, or red. The best known of these, today as in the past, is the Red Ensign. The old *Red Ensign,* shown here, was also known as the Meteor Flag, and widely used on ships during the colonial period.

The British *Royal Standard* is the personal flag of the British Sovereign and has been in use, in differing designs, for centuries. The pattern shown here is one of several employed during the seventeenth century. The smaller lions represent England; the larger lion, Scotland; the harp, Ireland; and the lilies, France.

Flags of the Revolution   2

The eighteenth century opened with a series of wars involving most of the European nations with their colonies in North America and elsewhere. These wars occupied much of the first half of the century and culminated in the Seven Years' War (1756-1763), the North American phase of which is usually referred to as the French and Indian War. Political and economic disputes continued to arise between Great Britain and her American colonies. These problems became increasingly more serious and far-reaching as the colonies grew and their economic interests enlarged. The defeat of the French at Quebec in 1759 with their subsequent expulsion from North America in 1763, at the conclusion of the Seven Years' War, removed a great danger to the British colonies. Furthermore, it enabled the more politically-minded of the colonists to turn their thoughts to consideration of imperial and local problems. A number of crises in colonial politics resulted. The most notable of these was the Stamp Act troubles of the 1760's. Eventually, these disagreements culminated in the Revolutionary struggle which began in earnest outside Boston in 1776 and continued until the British forces left the area in 1783. The Revolution was fought with relatively little central direction or organization and as a result most of the troops felt their loyalties belonged chiefly to the state or district from which they hailed. Consequently, the Revolution gave rise to a large number of flags, most of which had naval or military associations.

COMMANDER-IN-CHIEF'S
PERSONAL FLAG

COMMANDER-IN-CHIEF'S
LIFE GUARD FLAG

CONQUER OR DIE

The *Commander-in-Chief's Personal Flag* has been suggested (along with a number of other sources) as being the origin of the field of stars in the Stars and Stripes. This flag was flown by General Washington during the winter encampment at Valley Forge.

General Washington had a *Life Guard* or personal guard which consisted of picked troops contributed by each colony represented in the Continental Army. The Life Guard carried this color.

AN APPEAL TO HEAVEN

WASHINGTON'S
CRUISERS ENSIGN

During 1775, General Washington fitted out a squadron of six warships at his own expense. These vessels, generally known as *Washington's Cruisers*, hoisted an ensign which was adapted from the well-known and long-used New England Pine Tree Flag. This flag was later modified slightly and adopted by the Massachusetts Navy, one of the naval forces organized by the revolting colonies.

RHODE ISLAND FLAG

Elsewhere in New England other forces were being assembled and prepared for the struggle, and flags were provided for them. *Rhode Island* troops adopted an attractive blue and white banner, which is the basis for Rhode Island's present state flag. This flag, which bears the famous motto "Hope," was carried by Rhode Island troops at the battles of Brandywine, Trenton and Yorktown.

CONTINENTAL FLAG

Although the coming of the Revolution caused the rejection of traditional British patterns for flags in many instances, the older patterns persisted to a surprising degree. In the so-called Continental Flag we have a version of the Red Ensign or Meteor Flag in use for so many years. A green New England pine tree was substituted for the Union Flag in the canton. The *Continental Flag* is believed to have been carried at the Battle of Bunker Hill. Another flag, also believed to have been carried at the Battle of *Bunker Hill*, which takes its name from that action, used as its base the British Blue Ensign. This is a British flag similar to the Red Ensign except that it has a blue field with the traditional New England pine tree added to the canton.

BUNKER HILL FLAG

GRAND UNION FLAG

The need for one flag to be used by the American forces and by the navy, in particular, became more and more apparent. To serve this need, the Grand Union Flag was adopted. The *Grand Union Flag,* a combination of British and Revolutionary elements, is remarkable for a strange and, thus far, unexplained fact: it appears to be the same as the ensign used for many years by the East India Company whose policies contributed to the outbreak of the Revolution! This flag served the United Colonies from January 1776, until the adoption of the first version of the Stars and Stripes on June 14, 1777. The Grand Union Flag was first raised over General Washington's Continental Army encampments at Cambridge and Somerville, outside Boston. It is, therefore, sometimes spoken of as the Cambridge Flag. Later it was flown from the Battery in New York and was generally used on both land and sea. It was not, however, normally carried by Revolutionary troops in the field; these carried their own state or regimental colors and standards.

John Paul Jones is believed to have raised the Grand Union Flag, personally, the first time it was hoisted on an American warship. This was the flagship of the fleet under the command of Esek Hopkins. On November 16, 1776, the American warship, "Andrew Doria," saluted a Dutch fort in the West Indies and was saluted in turn, thus bringing

CONTINENTAL NAVY JACK

the United Colonies a measure of international recognition.

Although the Grand Union Flag was the principal American naval ensign during the first phases of the Revolution, several versions of the "Rattlesnake Flag" are also closely identified with the Revolutionary naval forces. The rattlesnake had early in the war become a distinctive symbol of the American cause and frequently appeared with the motto "Dont Tread on Me." The *Continental Navy Jack* placed a crawling rattlesnake on a field of red and white stripes.

The *Gadsden Flag*, another of the "Rattlesnake Flags," was presented to the Continental Congress by Colonel Christopher Gadsden of South Carolina from whom it takes its name. It was used on Revolutionary warships as the captain's personal flag. In this instance the snake is coiled and menacing on a yellow field.

GADSDEN FLAG

DONT TREAD ON ME

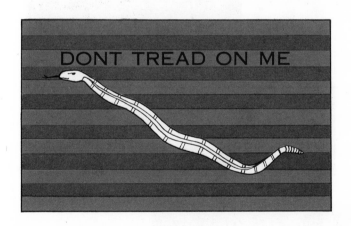

DONT TREAD ON ME

SOUTH CAROLINA
NAVY ENSIGN

A striking variation of the Rattlesnake Flag on which the patriotic snake is traveling across a field of red and blue stripes was employed for a time by the *South Carolina Navy*.

The relatively small size of the American naval forces resulted in the use of only a small number of naval flags. On land, however, the existence of many groups of local militia had the opposite effect, so we find a great variety of banners carried by the various military units. The *Liberty Tree Flag*, flown by a Boston patriot organization

LIBERTY TREE

AN APPEAL TO GOD

LIBERTY TREE
FLAG

called the Sons of Liberty, takes its name from the "Liberty Tree" in Boston which was cut down by General Gage's British troops in 1776. The Sons of Liberty had been in the habit of meeting under this tree. When it was cut down, it immediately became a symbol of resistance to British rule in Massachusetts. It appears as the central device on this flag used for a time during 1776.

LINKED HAND
FLAG

NEWBURY FLAG

TAUNTON FLAG

Another flag of local significance about which little is known is the *Linked Hand Flag*. This banner of unusual design is typical of the many improvised flags used by Revolutionary troops. A pleasing combination of red, white, and green was adopted by the people of the seaport town of *Newbury*, Massachusetts, for the flag which they hoisted during the early years of the Revolution. In another part of Massachusetts, however, the people of *Taunton* adapted the British Red Ensign to their purpose merely by adding "Liberty" to the field of that famous flag.

Although comparatively little serious fighting took place throughout most of New England, a significant battle occurred in New York State and part of what is now Vermont, on August 16, 1777. The Battle of *Bennington*, which helped to disrupt the British invasion of New York from Canada, was fought largely by Vermont militia who carried this early and elaborate version of the Stars and Stripes.

BENNINGTON FLAG

NEW YORK
ENSIGN

THIRD MARYLAND REGIMENT

As we move southward from New England, we find flags of different styles adopted in different areas. In 1775 *New York* adopted an *ensign* for its ships which bears a beaver on a white field, an allusion to the once-important fur trade of New York. The *Third Maryland Regiment* bore a color which closely resembles the first version of the Stars and Stripes adopted by the Continental Congress. This flag was carried by the Third Maryland Regiment at the Battle of Cowpens in South Carolina on January 17, 1781 and is one of the comparatively few variations of the Stars and Stripes which were carried in battle by Revolutionary troops.

The Revolutionary rattlesnake appears again, this time coiled and threatening, on a white field of the flag carried by the *Culpeper* Minute Men, a Virginia militia force.

The *Guilford Flag*, however, is another form of the Stars and Stripes although this fact is nearly concealed by the unusual selection of colors.

GUILFORD FLAG

The Guilford Flag, raised over Guilford Court House, North Carolina, on March 15, 1781, is a remarkable example of the lack of uniformity prevalent in the designing of flags during the Revolutionary period. Each local group made its own decision as to the flag to be used as its standard.

Two new flags had appeared at sea. One of these, the *Texel Flag*, is believed to have been designed by Benjamin Franklin and is also thought to have been flown by John Paul Jones during the famous

CULPEPER FLAG

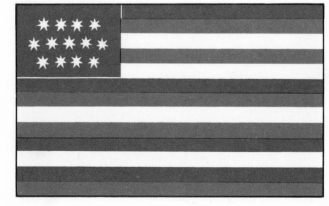

TEXEL FLAG

battle between the "Bon Homme Richard" and H.M.S. "Serapis." The flag takes its name from the Dutch island of Texel, for it is only from records preserved there that we have any knowledge of its design.

Meanwhile, American privateers and merchantmen continued to follow the British practice of flying an ensign different from that used by naval vessels. This flag generally showed the usual thirteen stripes but sometimes varied in color according to the fancy of the ship's captain. The *merchant flag* shown here continued in use until about 1795.

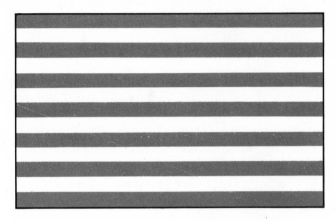

MERCHANT FLAG

The Revolutionary leaders eventually realized the need for a distinctive American flag. Consequently, after endless delay and much discussion, the *First Stars and Stripes* was adopted on June 14, 1777, by a resolution of the Continental Congress. This resolution stated: "That the flag of the thirteen United States be thirteen stripes, alternately red and white, that the union be thirteen stars, white in a blue field, representing a new constellation." This is the version of the United States Flag as it is known to us, and its "birthday," June 14, is commemorated each year as "Flag Day." There is considerable doubt as to the origin of the design of the flag. A number of suggestions have been advanced, but there is not enough evidence available to resolve the question. The oft-repeated story that Betsy Ross, a Philadelphia seamstress, designed and made the first flag of this pattern has never been verified, nor have the claims to that honor for Francis Hopkinson, a well-known colonial political leader from New Jersey. The Stars and Stripes saw action at sea during the latter part of the year 1777. On February 14, 1778, an American warship flying this new flag was saluted by a French fleet lying in Quiberon Bay on the coast of France, thus

STARS AND STRIPES (FIRST)

indicating a degree of international recognition for the United Colonies and their new flag. Legend has it that the symbolism of this flag was described by General George Washington, in these words: "We take the stars from heaven, the red from our mother country, separating it by white stripes, thus showing that we have separated from her, and the white stripes shall go down to posterity representing liberty."

The Stars and Stripes, therefore, was born in the midst of combat; it was the banner of a people in travail, giving birth to a new nation founded upon liberty and freedom.

The spirit of our flag is dramatically presented by Thomas Jefferson in this impassioned sentence: "I swear, before the altar of God, eternal hostility to every form of tyranny over the mind of man."

The early history of the Stars and Stripes is obscure, its first use on land was probably sometime in 1777. Nevertheless, as was the case with the Grand Union Flag, the land forces did not usually carry the Stars and Stripes but used their own local or regimental flags.

From among a large number of local and regimental flags, only a comparatively small number have survived. Among these is the standard of the *First Pennsylvania Rifle Regiment*. This regiment served, during the course of the Revolution, in each of the thirteen colonies,

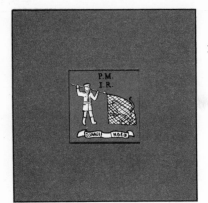

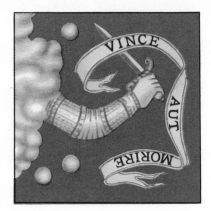

FIRST PENNSYLVANIA RIFLE REGIMENT

BEDFORD FLAG

and its distinctive banner was carried at the significant battles of Trenton, Princeton, Brandywine, Monmouth and Yorktown.

The *Bedford Flag*, carried by the Bedford Minute Men at the Battle of Concord, is perhaps the most interesting in appearance of all the Revolutionary flags. It bears a striking resemblance to the much older standard of the Three County Troop.

The ornate standard of the fashionable Philadelphia Troop of Light Horse (that is, light cavalry) is one of the earlier flags to carry a design of thirteen stripes. The *Philadelphia Light Horse* acted as escort to General Washington on his trip from Philadelphia to Cambridge in 1775, to take command of the Continental Army.

PHILADELPHIA LIGHT HORSE STANDARD

PULASKI'S FLAG

The Polish adventurer and patriot, Count Casimir *Pulaski,* raised his own corps of infantry and cavalry. They fought with distinction at the Battle of Brandywine and at the Siege of Savannah, during which encounter the Count was killed. His troops fought under this unusual flag.

NEW YORK REGIMENT'S COLORS

The striking color of the *New York Regiment,* consisting of that state's coat of arms on a blue field, was made during 1778 or 1779 and carried by New York troops at the Battle of Yorktown. This flag is the basis for New York's modern state flag. An attractive standard was carried by *Tallmadge's Dragoons* at the battles of Brandywine, Germantown and Monmouth. This flag is notable for the arrangement of thirteen stripes in the canton.

PROVIDENCE ARTILLERY COLOR

TALLMADGE'S DRAGOONS

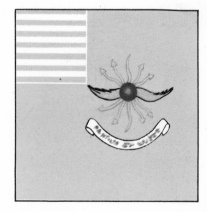

HULBERT FLAG

EASTON FLAG

In April 1775, a Rhode Island militia unit, the *Providence Artillery*, adopted a remarkable banner displaying a number of widely used Revolutionary symbols, including the coiled rattlesnake with his warning motto and an array of thirteen stars.

John *Hulbert*, a Long Island militia officer, reputedly prepared this flag in 1776. Although little has been established about the actual history of the flag, it seems to place Captain Hulbert in the running for the distinction of having designed the Stars and Stripes.

A curious flag which hails from Easton, Pennsylvania, and which contains all the elements of the Stars and Stripes arranged in a rather unusual manner, has also been claimed as the origin of the Stars and Stripes. It appears, however, that in actual fact the *Easton Flag* did not figure in the Revolution at all, but arrived on the scene during the War of 1812 at which time it was carried by a militia unit from Easton.

The *French Army* which came to the aid of the American forces in 1779 carried its own separate *banners*. Three of its flags are shown

 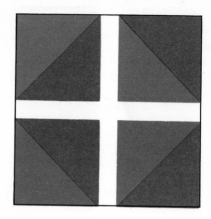

FRENCH REGIMENTAL FLAGS

here. Each of the regiments carrying these flags, together with other units of the French army, served with distinction during the latter part of the Revolution; they were all present at the Battle of Yorktown. The colors in the flags are basically the white flag of France with bold designs painted on the white field to produce very striking emblems.

A number of regiments of German troops were employed by the British Government during the Revolution. One of these regiments came from the German Principality of *Ansbach* or Anspach, and carried this rather interesting banner. The flag fell into the hands of American troops at the Battle of Yorktown.

The flag of the *Second New Hampshire Regiment* was carried until it was lost to a British force shortly before the Battle of Saratoga. It will be seen that it retains a small British Union Flag in its canton.

This extraordinary flag was carried by Colonel William Washington at the battles of Cowpens and *Eutaw* Springs in South Carolina. The

☆ **45**

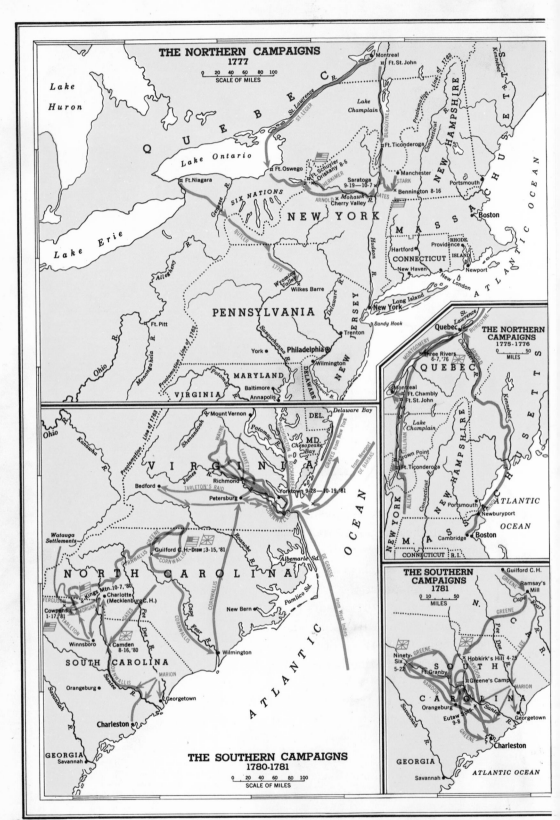

THE NORTHERN CAMPAIGNS
1777

SCALE OF MILES
0 20 40 60 80 100

Lake Huron

QUEBEC

St. Lawrence R.

Montreal
Ft. St. John

ST. LEGER

Lake Ontario

Ft. Oswego

Ft. Niagara

Genesee R.

SIX NATIONS

HERKIMER

Schuyler
Oriskany 8-6

Cherry Valley

Mohawk R.

ARNOLD

Lake Champlain

BURGOYNE

Ft. Ticonderoga

Saratoga
9-19 — 10-7

GATES

STARK

Bennington 8-16

Manchester

NEW HAMPSHIRE

Portsmouth

MASSACHUSETTS

Boston

ATLANTIC OCEAN

Proclamation Line of 1768

NEW YORK

Lake Erie

Allegheny R.

BUTLER

1778

Wyoming Valley

Wilkes Barre

Delaware R.

Hudson R.

Hartford

RHODE ISLAND

Providence

CONNECTICUT

New Haven

Newport

New London

Ft. Pitt

PENNSYLVANIA

Susquehanna R.

Monongahela R.

Ohio R.

York

Philadelphia

Proclamation Line of 1768

Trenton

NEW JERSEY

New York

Long Island

Sandy Hook

Wilmington

MARYLAND

Delaware B.

VIRGINIA

Baltimore

Annapolis

THE NORTHERN CAMPAIGNS
1775-1776

MILES
0   50

St. Lawrence R.

Quebec

BURGOYNE

ARNOLD

MONTGOMERY

Three Rivers
6-7, '76

QUEBEC

Montreal
Ft. Chambly
Ft. St. John

Lake Champlain

Kennebec R.

SULLIVAN

Town Point

Ft. Ticonderoga

NEW HAMPSHIRE

NEW YORK

Portsmouth

Newburyport

ATLANTIC OCEAN

ALLEN

Connecticut R.

MASSACHUSETTS

Cambridge

Boston

CONNECTICUT

R.I.

Ohio R.

Kanawha R.

Mount Vernon

Shenandoah R.

WAYNE

Proclamation Line of 1768

VIRGINIA

Potomac R.

James R.

Richmond

Bedford

TARLETON'S RAID

Petersburg

LAFAYETTE

MD.
Chesapeake Bay

Potomac R.

DEL.

Delaware Bay

GRAVES from New York

DE BARRAS from Newport

Yorktown 9-28 — 10-19, '81

CORNWALLIS

WASHINGTON & ROCHAMBEAU

ATLANTIC OCEAN

DE GRASSE from West Indies

Watauga Settlements

GREENE

CORNWALLIS

Guilford C.H.—Draw; 3-15, '81

Roanoke R.

Albemarle Sd.

NORTH CAROLINA

GATES

FERGUSON

Kings Mtn. 10-7, '80

MORGAN

Charlotte
(Mecklenburg C.H.)

TARLETON

Cowpens
1-17, '81

Winnsboro

Camden
8-16, '80

CORNWALLIS

Pee Dee R.

Cape Fear R.

New Bern

Pamlico Sd.

Wilmington

SOUTH CAROLINA

Santee R.

MARION

Orangeburg

Georgetown

Savannah R.

Charleston

GEORGIA

Savannah

ATLANTIC

THE SOUTHERN CAMPAIGNS
1780-1781

SCALE OF MILES
0 20 40 60 80 100

THE SOUTHERN CAMPAIGNS
1781

MILES
0 10   50

Guilford C.H.

GREENE

Ramsay's Mill

Cape Fear R.

N. CAR.

GREENE

Pee Dee R.

Ninety-Six
5-22

GREENE

Ft. Granby

Hobkirk's Hill 4-25

Greene's Camp

SOUTH

Orangeburg

RAWDON

Eutaw Spgs.
9-8

Santee R.

CAROLINA

MARION

Georgetown

Savannah R.

Charleston

GEORGIA

Savannah

ATLANTIC OCEAN

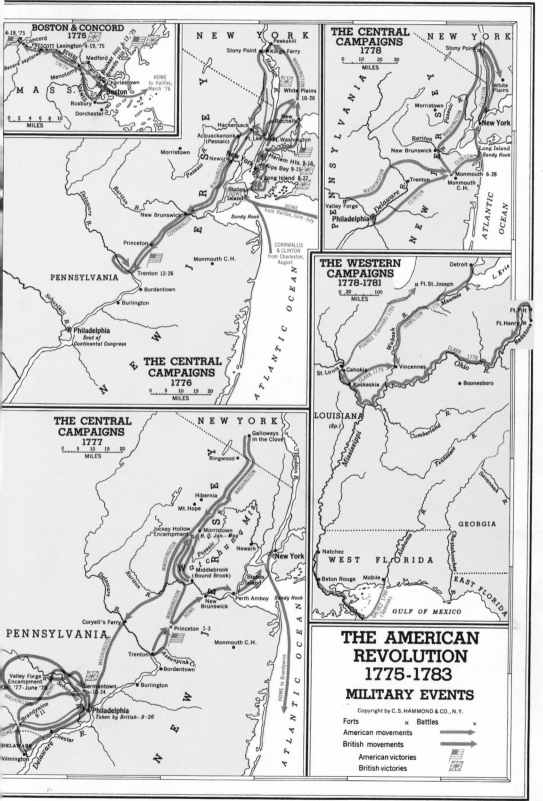

BOSTON & CONCORD 1775
4-19, '75
Concord
PRESCOTT Lexington 4-19, '75
Revere captured
BEVERLEY
Medford
SMITH
Menotomy
Charlestown Bunker Hill 6-17, '75
Breeds Hill
DAWES
Roxbury
Boston
Dorchester
MASS.
HOWE to Halifax, March '76
0 2 4 6 8 10
MILES

THE CENTRAL CAMPAIGNS 1776
NEW YORK
Stony Point Peekskill
Kings Ferry
Hudson R.
White Plains 10-28
WASHINGTON
New Rochelle
Hackensack
Acquackanonk (Passaic)
Ft. Lee Ft. Washington
Morristown
Newark New York
Passaic R.
Harlem Hts. 9-16
Kips Bay 9-15
Long Island 8-27
Staten Island
HOWE
HOWE from Halifax, June-July
New Brunswick
Raritan R.
Sandy Hook
CORNWALLIS
CORNWALLIS & CLINTON from Charleston, August
Princeton
JERSEY
Monmouth C.H.
PENNSYLVANIA
Trenton 12-26
Bordentown
Burlington
Delaware R.
Schuylkill R.
Philadelphia
Seat of Continental Congress
N
0 5 10 15 20
MILES

THE CENTRAL CAMPAIGNS 1778
NEW YORK
Stony Point
0 10 20 30
MILES
Morristown
Passaic R.
CLINTON
White Plains
WASHINGTON
New York
Raritan
Long Island
Sandy Hook
New Brunswick
CLINTON
Trenton
Monmouth 6-28
Monmouth C.H.
Valley Forge
Delaware R.
Philadelphia
NEW JERSEY
ATLANTIC OCEAN

THE WESTERN CAMPAIGNS 1778-1781
Detroit
L. Erie
Ft. St. Joseph
0 20 100
MILES
Maumee R.
HAMILTON 1778
Ft. Pitt
Ft. Henry
Redstone
POUREE (Spanish) 1781
Wabash R.
CLARK 1778
Ohio R.
St. Louis Cahokia
CLARK 1779 Vincennes
Kaskaskia
Boonesboro
LOUISIANA (Sp.)
Mississippi R.
Cumberland R.
Tennessee R.
Savannah R.
GEORGIA
Natchez
WEST FLORIDA
Alabama R.
Chattahoochee R.
Baton Rouge Mobile
EAST FLORIDA
GALVEZ 1780 (Spanish)
GULF OF MEXICO

THE CENTRAL CAMPAIGNS 1777
NEW YORK
0 5 10 15 20
MILES
Galloways in the Clove
Ringwood
Hudson R.
Hibernia
Mt. Hope
WASHINGTON
Jockey Hollow Encampment
Morristown H.Q. Jan.-May
Passaic R.
Newark
New York
Watchung Mts.
Middlebrook (Bound Brook)
Staten Island
WASHINGTON
HOWE
New Brunswick
Perth Amboy
Sandy Hook
Coryell's Ferry
Delaware R.
Raritan R.
Princeton 1-3
Monmouth C.H.
PENNSYLVANIA
Trenton
Assunpink Cr.
Bordentown
Valley Forge Encampment Dec. '77-June '78
WASHINGTON
HOWE to Brandywine
Germantown 10-24
Burlington
Schuylkill R.
HOWE
Brandywine 9-11
Philadelphia
Taken by British - 9-26
DELAWARE
Chester
Delaware R.
Wilmington
NEW JERSEY
ATLANTIC OCEAN

THE AMERICAN REVOLUTION 1775-1783
MILITARY EVENTS
Copyright by C.S. HAMMOND & CO., N.Y.

Forts	¤ Battles ×
American movements	→
British movements	→
American victories	
British victories	

ANSBACH FLAG

SECOND NEW HAMPSHIRE
REGIMENT

EUTAW STANDARD

flag was, according to legend, hastily made by Colonel Washington's fiancée from the upholstery of a drawing room chair!

Pennsylvania's *Westmoreland County Battalion* was raised in 1776 and adopted as its color that old stand-by, the British Red Ensign, to which were added the familiar coiled rattlesnake and the motto "Dont Tread on Me."

In September 1775, *Colonel Moultrie* of South Carolina devised a flag for the troops under his command. The Fort Moultrie Flag, which has the word "Liberty" added to the lower part of the field, was flown at the Battle of Charleston, June 28, 1776, when the gallant defense

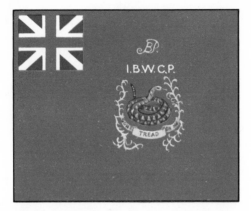

WESTMORELAND COUNTY BATTALION

MOULTRIE'S FLAG

of Fort Sullivan by Colonel Moultrie and the force under his command prevented the British occupation of Charleston. These flags are the basis of the South Carolina State Flag adopted at the beginning of the Civil War and still in use.

3 Post-Revolutionary Flags

With the successful outcome of the Revolution for the American colonies, the Treaty of Paris was concluded in 1783. This treaty recognized the independence of the United States and established the boundaries of the new nation. The large variety of flags which had flown during the war rapidly disappeared, leaving the Stars and Stripes as a lasting addition to the world's array of national banners.

The United States arrived on the international scene a short time before the outbreak of the French Revolution and the almost endless series of Napoleonic Wars which followed. It soon found itself in a world seething with political rivalry and intrigue. Although the Government sought generally to steer clear of "foreign entanglements," nevertheless, many questions had to be negotiated with Great Britain, France, Spain and lesser powers. These negotiations loom large in the history of the early decades of the country's existence as a newly independent nation.

In the early years of the nineteenth century, therefore, a number of other flags played varying roles in American history. The first of these is the *French Tricolor*. The traditional flags of France, the "lily banner" of gold fleurs-de-lis on a blue field and the plain white Bourbon flag, were swept away in the Revolution which began in 1793 and continued until the rise of Napoleon to power. The new flag, entirely different from its predecessors, waved over French Louisiana until the cession of that huge territory to the United States in 1803.

FRENCH TRICOLOR

RUSSIAN-AMERICAN COMPANY'S FLAG

While France was withdrawing from the North American continent, Russia was expanding her foothold here. The *Russian-American Company*, which colonized and administered Alaska for the Russian Empire and which also had an outpost in northern California for a number of years, used the flag shown until 1867, when Alaska was sold to the United States. Another *Russian* flag, the *ensign* of the

RUSSIAN ENSIGN

Czarist navy, also fluttered in Alaskan waters until 1867. This flag is a variation of the same Cross of St. Andrew which, in its conventional form, is the Scottish national flag.

With the passage of time, new states were admitted to the Union. This disturbed the plan employed in designing the Stars and Stripes whereby each state of the Union was represented by one star and one

STARS AND STRIPES (FIFTEEN STRIPES)

stripe. On January 13, 1794, therefore, Congress passed an act providing that after May 1, 1795, the National Flag should have fifteen stars and fifteen stripes, the additional stars and stripes to represent the recently admitted states of Vermont and Kentucky. This flag was used for the next twenty-three years and is sometimes referred to as the *Flag of Fifteen Stripes*. It was used during the Tripoli Expedition of 1805 and the War of 1812 and is, therefore, the "Star-Spangled Banner" of our National Anthem.

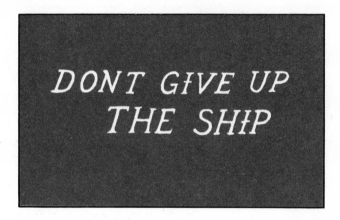

PERRY'S FLAG

The second war with Great Britain, the War of 1812, did not produce as many flags as did the Revolutionary War. One unusual flag was, however, used at the Battle of Lake Erie on September 10, 1813. Commodore Oliver Hazard Perry, in command of an improvised American squadron, hoisted this flag. The quotation "Dont Give Up the Ship" recalls the words of Captain James Lawrence, the hero of an earlier naval encounter near Boston. However, the flag has become known as *Commodore Perry's Flag*.

Soon it became evident that the addition of another stripe to the flag for every new state would create hopeless confusion. Accordingly, in *1818*, Congress passed an act providing that after July 4th of that year the flag would show thirteen stripes and twenty stars, and that in the future a new star but no new stripe would be added for each new state admitted to the Union. This is the practice which has been followed since then.

It should be noted here that the United States Army did not carry the Stars and Stripes in the field during the earlier years of the country's history although the army did fly the Stars and Stripes as a garrison flag. The use of the National Flag was not authorized for the artillery

STARS AND STRIPES (1818)

until 1834, for the infantry until 1841, and for the cavalry until 1895. The Stars and Stripes was, therefore, first regularly carried by troops in battle during the Mexican War (1846-1848).

During the 1820's and 1830's numbers of Americans emigrated to Texas and settled down in that Mexican state. The growing population of American settlers in Texas and differences between them and the Mexican Government led finally to the Texan War of Independence

ALAMO FLAG

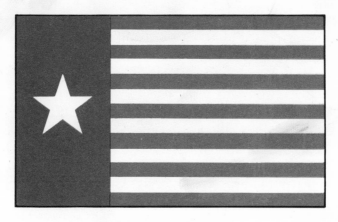

TEXAS NAVAL ENSIGN

which culminated in the Battle of San Jacinto and the establishment of the independent Republic of Texas.

The defenders of the *Alamo* in San Antonio conducted their epic defense of the Texan stronghold under a modified version of the Mexican National Flag. The date 1824 in the white stripe indicates the adherence of the Texans to the Mexican constitution of 1824.

The Republic of Texas adopted two flags. The first, the *Texas*

TEXAS NATIONAL FLAG

Naval Ensign, was adopted on April 9, 1836 for use by the Texas Navy. It was obviously copied from the United States Flag and preceded the *Texas National Flag* by several months. The latter has been used since 1836, first as a national flag and later as a state flag, without change.

The tide of westward expansion carried American settlers into another Mexican territory, California, during the 1840's. A local uprising of Americans in California during 1846 resulted in the establishment of a short-lived republic which adopted a flag. The *Bear Flag* has been in use intermittently ever since, having been adopted as California's state flag in 1911. It is unusual both in its design and in its use of the word "Republic" to describe the State of California.

BEAR FLAG

In 1815, after the termination of the War of 1812, the United States entered a period of relative quiet and growth which lasted for a number of years. Times of peace and prosperity are seldom marked by the events which give rise to flags and other symbols of nationality. During this period the Stars and Stripes gradually accumulated new stars as additional states were created and admitted to the Union. Finally, however, in 1846, the United States went to war with Mexico over the disputed boundary between Texas and Mexico. So fast were new states being added to the Union that the short *Mexican War* (1846-1848) was conducted under three different forms of the Stars and Stripes. The last of these, bearing twenty-nine stars, is shown here.

One of the few distinctive flags devised during this period is the rather striking version of the national colors carried by General John Frémont on his wide-spread explorations in the Far West during the 1840's. As the army did not normally carry the National Flag during this period, *General Frémont's Flag* was especially prepared for his expeditions.

MEXICAN WAR FLAG

The period between the Mexican War and the Civil War, which began in 1861, is distinguished by little more than the addition of new stars for new states.

FRÉMONT'S FLAG

4   *Civil War Flags*

As the nation expanded westward, tensions began to develop between the older states of the East and those in the South. The rapid industrialization and economic growth of the Northeastern states was in marked contrast to the development of the predominantly agricultural South. Differences increased steadily over the years, especially on the issue of slavery. This question gradually achieved gigantic proportions, with many diverse and complex factors. These factors finally combined and exploded in the great crisis of American history — the Civil War.

Whereas the Revolution produced a large number of local, transitory flags, the Civil War did not. The greater complexity of society and the more systematic organization of military forces did not allow much scope for the exercise of local or private initiative in providing emblems for the troops involved. A number of Northern volunteer regiments did, however, carry colors which were in later years adopted as state flags by their home states. The battle flag of the Confederacy, discussed in detail further in this chapter, is the one lasting contribution of the Civil War to history's stock of flags. This flag, as well-known today as it was in 1865, has long outlived the circumstances which created it.

At the beginning of the Civil War it was suggested to President Lincoln that the existing national flag should be divided diagonally in half, the North using the upper portion and making the lower portion

STARS AND STRIPES (CIVIL WAR FLAG)

white, while the Confederacy would use the opposite arrangement.
Neither side thought very much of this idea, however. The Union
retained the full number of stars, contrary to another suggestion that
the stars representing the seceded states should be removed. In fact,
two stars were added to the thirty-four on the flag in 1861. The flag
shown here is the *thirty-six star version* in use during the last year of
the Civil War.

South Carolina, the first of the Southern states to secede, adopted

PALMETTO FLAG

early in 1861 the *Palmetto Flag* which served that state during its brief period of independence, during its period as a member of the Confederacy, and then again as a state from the end of the Civil War to the present day.

While the Union continued to use the Stars and Stripes without alteration, the Confederacy found it necessary to provide itself with new and distinctive banners. Accordingly a number of flags were adopted by the Confederacy during its short but eventful history. The first of these, the famous *Stars and Bars,* was adopted in March 1861,

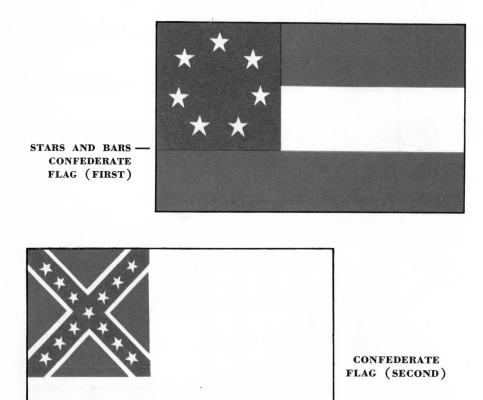

STARS AND BARS —
CONFEDERATE
FLAG (FIRST)

CONFEDERATE
FLAG (SECOND)

and continued in use until May 1863. The pattern and colors of this flag did not distinguish it sharply from the Stars and Stripes of the Union. Consequently, considerable confusion was caused on the battlefield. On May 1, 1863, therefore, a *second design* was adopted, placing the Battle Flag on a white field. This flag, however, was easily mistaken for a white flag of surrender, so on March 4, 1865, a short time before the collapse of the Confederacy, a *third pattern* was adopted; a broad bar of red was placed on the outer edge of the white field.

In addition, two naval flags were in use from 1861 until 1863. The *ensign* was similar to the "Stars and Bars" but with the stars in the canton arranged differently, while the *jack* was simply the canton of the national flag as it was used on land.

The best-known Confederate flag, however, was the *Battle Flag*, sometimes called the "Southern Cross," which was carried by Confederate troops in the field and also used as a jack at sea from 1863

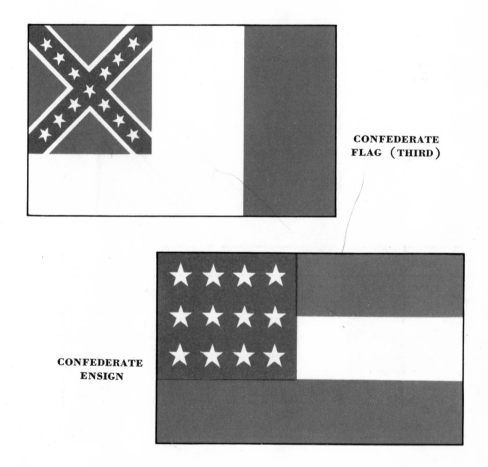

CONFEDERATE
FLAG (THIRD)

CONFEDERATE
ENSIGN

onward. This flag has become the generally recognized symbol of the South.

In addition to the officially adopted flags of the Confederacy, another flag, the so-called *Bonnie Blue Flag*, achieved some popularity in the South during 1861. Although not used by the Confederate Government, it became a well-known symbol of the Confederacy and

CONFEDERATE JACK

CONFEDERATE BATTLE FLAG

it inspired a popular song called the "Bonnie Blue Flag."

The spirit of secession, which burst into flame at the beginning of the War Between the States, was expressed in various forms during the next four years. One of these was the intense independence each Southern state determined to exhibit. Such sentiment was immediately manifest in the numerous flags used by the Confederate forces. Emblems were designed for many local groups as well as the separate

BONNIE BLUE FLAG

states. As a result, many colorful banners flew briefly over a people fighting fiercely for a cause in which they wholeheartedly believed. The six noted here are a partial representation.

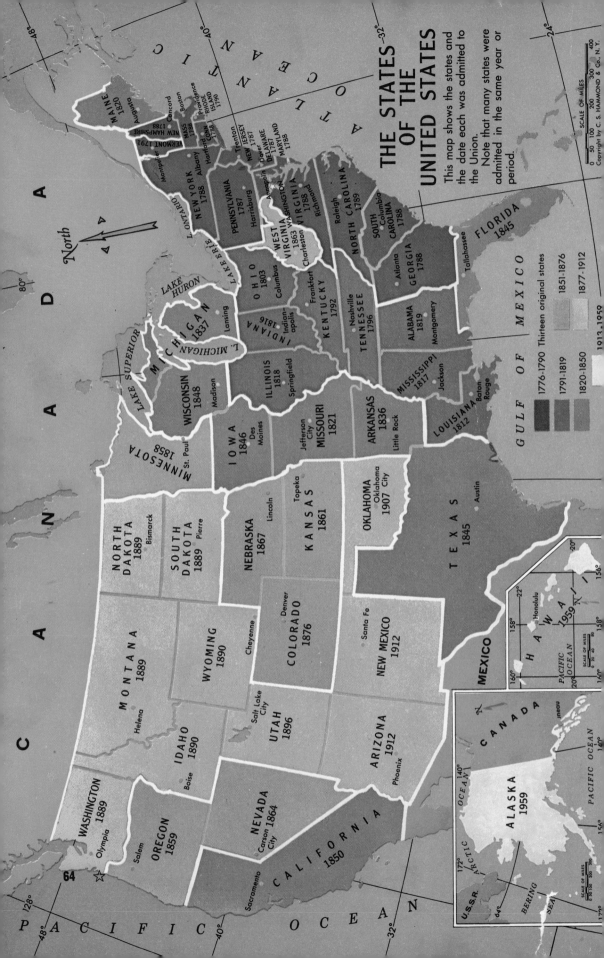

THE STATES OF THE UNITED STATES

This map shows the states and the date each was admitted to the Union.
Note that many states were admitted in the same year or period.

SCALE OF MILES

Copyright by C. S. HAMMOND & Co., N.Y.

1776-1790 Thirteen original states	1851-1876	
1791-1819	1877-1912	
1820-1850	1913-1959	

North

Atlantic Ocean

MAINE 1820 — Augusta
NEW HAMPSHIRE 1788 — Concord
VERMONT 1791 — Montpelier
MASS. 1788 — Boston
RHODE ISLAND 1790 — Providence
CONN. 1788 — Hartford
NEW YORK 1788 — Albany
NEW JERSEY 1787 — Trenton
PENNSYLVANIA 1787 — Harrisburg
DELAWARE 1787 — Dover
MARYLAND 1788 — Annapolis
WEST VIRGINIA 1863 — Charleston
VIRGINIA 1788 — Richmond — Washington
NORTH CAROLINA 1789 — Raleigh
SOUTH CAROLINA 1788 — Columbia
GEORGIA 1788 — Atlanta
FLORIDA 1845 — Tallahassee
OHIO 1803 — Columbus
KENTUCKY 1792 — Frankfort
TENNESSEE 1796 — Nashville
INDIANA 1816 — Indianapolis
ILLINOIS 1818 — Springfield
MICHIGAN 1837 — Lansing
ALABAMA 1819 — Montgomery
MISSISSIPPI 1817 — Jackson
LOUISIANA 1812 — Baton Rouge
ARKANSAS 1836 — Little Rock
MISSOURI 1821 — Jefferson City
IOWA 1846 — Des Moines
WISCONSIN 1848 — Madison
MINNESOTA 1858 — St. Paul

LAKE SUPERIOR — LAKE MICHIGAN — LAKE HURON — LAKE ERIE — LAKE ONTARIO

GULF OF MEXICO

NORTH DAKOTA 1889 — Bismarck
SOUTH DAKOTA 1889 — Pierre
NEBRASKA 1867 — Lincoln
KANSAS 1861 — Topeka
OKLAHOMA 1907 — Oklahoma City
TEXAS 1845 — Austin
MONTANA 1889 — Helena
WYOMING 1890 — Cheyenne
COLORADO 1876 — Denver
NEW MEXICO 1912 — Santa Fe
IDAHO 1890 — Boise
UTAH 1896 — Salt Lake City
ARIZONA 1912 — Phoenix
WASHINGTON 1889 — Olympia
OREGON 1859 — Salem
NEVADA 1864 — Carson City
CALIFORNIA 1850 — Sacramento

CANADA

MEXICO

PACIFIC OCEAN

HAWAII 1959 — Honolulu

ALASKA 1959 — Juneau
U.S.S.R. — BERING SEA — ARCTIC OCEAN — PACIFIC OCEAN — CANADA

64

Flags Since the Civil War 5

The collapse of the Confederacy in 1865 closed the military phase of the Civil War. A new era began — an era as tragic in its own way as the period of fighting had been. The devastation of five years of internal fighting bringing distress, death and destruction could not be quickly mended. Between the victor and the vanquished there existed a deep gulf of bitterness and mistrust.

The outcome of the war established a strong central government instead of individual sovereign states, thereby saving the Union. Secession was outlawed and the slaves were freed. Manufacturing had prospered in the North during the war and this prosperity continued after Lee's surrender. The nation's material wealth multiplied with business becoming an important factor in the industrial expansion.

Most of the territories beyond the Mississippi achieved statehood before 1900, which increased their contribution to the national economy. The country prospered. American interests were primarily national with little thought for the countries beyond our shores. Around 1890, however, the United States began moving away from this idea of isolation. It wanted more markets for the products of its expanding industries. It wanted more influence in world politics. Most of all, it wanted to take its place among the great nations. Finally, it was the war with Spain in 1898 which marked the entrance of the United States on the international stage.

The Spanish-American War was fought under the *forty-five star*

STARS AND STRIPES (SPANISH-AMERICAN WAR FLAG)

banner which had been adopted in 1896, on the admission of Utah to the Union. It continued in use until 1908.

During the Spanish-American War, although not as a result of it, the United States acquired the Pacific island chain of Hawaii. The *Flag of Hawaii*, adopted originally by the independent Kingdom of Hawaii early in the nineteenth century, is remarkable for its use of the British Union Flag as its canton and for the bold pattern of stripes in its field. This flag has served the Kingdom, Territory and now the State of Hawaii as a distinctive and eye-catching emblem. The use of

HAWAIIAN FLAG

the British flag as part of the Hawaiian flag is believed to stem from the impression made upon an Hawaiian king by Captain Vancouver, the British explorer, who presented a Union Jack to King Kamehameha in 1791.

The *forty-eight star version* of the Stars and Stripes is rather remarkable for its long career beginning in 1912, with the admission of New Mexico and Arizona to the Union, and continuing until 1959 with the admission of Alaska. It is this flag to which President Wilson referred in his 1917 Flag Day message when he said:

"This flag, which we honor and under which we serve, is the emblem of our unity, our power, our thought and purpose as a nation. It has no other character than that which we give it from generation to generation. The choices are ours. It floats in majestic silence above the hosts that execute those choices, whether in peace or in war. And yet, though silent, it speaks to us — speaks to us of the past, of the men and women who went before us, and of the records they wrote upon it.

"We celebrate the day of its birth; and from its birth until now it has witnessed a great history, has floated on high the symbol of great events, of a great plan of life worked out by a great people . . .

STARS AND STRIPES (FORTY-EIGHT STARS)

"Woe be to the man or group of men that seeks to stand in our way in this day of high resolution when every principle we hold dearest is to be vindicated and made secure for the salvation of the nation. We are ready to plead at the bar of history, and our flag shall wear a new luster. Once more we shall make good with our lives and fortunes the great faith to which we were born, and a new glory shall shine in the face of our people."

ALASKAN FLAG

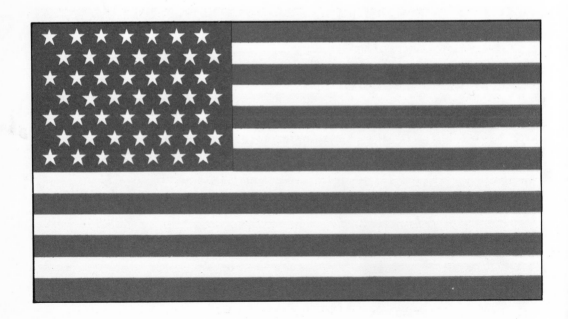

STARS AND STRIPES (FORTY-NINE STARS)

STARS AND STRIPES (FIFTY STARS)

Alaska's flag was adopted in a rather interesting manner. During 1927 a contest was held in the public schools of *Alaska* for a design for the territorial flag. The successful pattern was submitted by a thirteen-year-old seventh grade pupil from Seward. The design went into use shortly thereafter as Alaska's territorial flag and has now become the state flag of the forty-ninth state.

The *forty-nine star flag* had a very short life — one year — serving from 1959 until 1960 when it was superseded in turn by the present *fifty-star flag* which came into use on the admission of Hawaii as a state of the Union.

The practice, which originated in 1818, of adding a star to the flag for every newly created state has continued to the present day and has resulted in the flag in use at the present time. The admission of Hawaii to the Union in 1960 produced the flag shown here which came into use officially on July 4, 1960. Thus, in a little less than two hundred years, the Stars and Stripes has increased its constellation from thirteen to fifty bright and shining stars. In so doing, it has reflected the story of the American Union which has prospered and grown from a small beginning of thirteen colonies along the Atlantic seacoast to its present wealth and power, comprising fifty states which extend from ocean to ocean and beyond.

☆ **69**

The following table traces changes in the United States flag since 1777:

DATE OF DESIGN	NUMBER OF STARS	NEW STATES
JUNE 14, 1777	13	ORIGINAL THIRTEEN
MAY 1, 1795	15	VERMONT, KENTUCKY
JULY 4, 1818	20	TENNESSEE, OHIO, LOUISIANA, INDIANA, MISSISSIPPI
JULY 4, 1819	21	ILLINOIS
JULY 4, 1820	23	ALABAMA, MAINE
JULY 4, 1822	24	MISSOURI
JULY 4, 1836	25	ARKANSAS
JULY 4, 1837	26	MICHIGAN
JULY 4, 1845	27	FLORIDA
JULY 4, 1846	28	TEXAS
JULY 4, 1847	29	IOWA
JULY 4, 1848	30	WISCONSIN
JULY 4, 1851	31	CALIFORNIA
JULY 4, 1858	32	MINNESOTA
JULY 4, 1859	33	OREGON
JULY 4, 1861	34	KANSAS
JULY 4, 1863	35	WEST VIRGINIA
JULY 4, 1865	36	NEVADA
JULY 4, 1867	37	NEBRASKA
JULY 4, 1876	38	COLORADO
JULY 4, 1890	43	NORTH DAKOTA, SOUTH DAKOTA, MONTANA, WASHINGTON, IDAHO
JULY 4, 1891	44	WYOMING
JULY 4, 1896	45	UTAH
JULY 4, 1908	46	OKLAHOMA
JULY 4, 1912	48	NEW MEXICO, ARIZONA
JULY 4, 1959	49	ALASKA
JULY 4, 1960	50	HAWAII

PRESIDENT'S FLAG

A number of other flags are in use in the United States. One of these is the *President's Flag*. A distinctive presidential flag, flown only in the presence of the President of the United States, has been in use in different designs for many years. The present pattern includes stars recently added to represent Alaska and Hawaii. The President's Flag presents an appearance both pleasing and dramatic.

UNITED STATES
JACK

The *United States Jack* (or, more formally, the Union Jack —
not to be confused with the British Union Flag or "Union Jack") is
a small flag usually flown from the bow of warships and, occasionally,
by other vessels while at anchor or when dressed with flags for holidays
and celebrations. The jack is also used as a flag of office by diplomatic
officers and the governors of insular possessions of the United States
while they are on board ship. The jack is, in reality, the field of stars
taken from the National Flag; hence the name "Union Jack." The
number of stars on the jack has, of course, increased as the number of
stars on the Stars and Stripes has grown.

A striking and unusual flag is the ensign of the United States
Coast Guard. This vertically striped flag was adopted in 1799 and has
continued in use with minor changes to the present. It is the oldest
service flag still in use in the United States. This flag, without the
badge in the field, is also employed as the United States Customs Flag.
The vertical stripes present an eye-catching and easily remembered
pattern.

Flag Code

SOURCE: UNITED STATES CODE, 1958 ED., TITLE 36, CH. 10, SECTIONS 171-178.

§ 171. (National anthem); conduct during playing.

When the national anthem is played and the flag is not displayed, all present should stand and face toward the music. Those in uniform should salute at the first note of the anthem, retaining this position until the last note. All others should stand at attention, men removing the headdress. When the flag is displayed, all present should face the flag and salute.

(June 22, 1942, ch. 435, § 6, 56 Stat. 380; Dec. 22, 1942, ch. 806, § 6, 56 Stat. 1077.)

AMENDMENTS

1942 — Act Dec. 22, 1942, substituted "all present should face the flag and salute," in last sentence, for "the salute to the flag should be given."

§ 172. Pledge of allegiance to the flag; manner of delivery.

The following is designated as the pledge of allegiance to the flag: "I pledge allegiance to the flag of the United States of America and to the Republic for which it stands, one Nation under God, indivisible, with liberty and justice for all." Such pledge should be rendered by standing with the right hand over the heart. However, civilians will always show full respect to the flag when the pledge is given by merely standing at attention, men removing the headdress. Persons in uniform shall render the military salute.

(June 22, 1942, ch. 435, § 6, 56 Stat. 380; Dec. 22, 1942, ch. 806, § 6, 56 Stat. 1077.) Dec. 28, 1945, ch. 607, 59 Stat. 668; June 14, 1954, ch. 297, 68 Stat. 249.)

AMENDMENTS

1954 — Act June 14, 1954, amended section by inserting "under God," in the pledge.

1945 — Act Dec. 28, 1945, amended section by inserting "The following is designated as," inserting period after "justice for all." and deleting "is rendered by standing with the right hand over the heart." in the first sentence, and by inserting second sentence "Such pledge should * * * "

1942 — Act Dec. 22, 1942, deleted words: "extending the right hand, palm upward, toward the flag at the words 'to the flag' and holding this position until the end, when the hand drops to the side.", at end of first sentence.

§ 173. Display and use of flag by civilians; codification of rules and customs.

The following codification of existing rules and customs pertaining to the display and use of the flag of the United States of America is established for the use of such civilians or civilian groups or organizations as may not be required to conform with regulations promulgated by one or more executive departments of the Government of the United States.

(June 22, 1942, ch. 435, § 1, 56 Stat. 377; Dec. 22, 1942, ch. 806, § 1, 56 Stat. 1074.)

AMENDMENTS

1942 — Act Dec. 22, 1942, reenacted section without change.

§ 174. Same; time and occasions for display; hoisting and lowering.

(a) It is the universal custom to display the flag only from sunrise to sunset on buildings and on stationary flagstaffs in the open. However, the flag may be displayed at night upon special occasions when it is desired to produce a patriotic effect.

(b) The flag should be hoisted briskly and lowered ceremoniously.

(c) The flag should not be displayed on days when the weather is inclement.

(d) The flag should be displayed on all days when the weather permits, especially on New Year's Day, January 1; Inauguration Day, January 20; Lincoln's Birthday, February 12; Washington's Birthday, February 22; Army Day, April 6; Easter Sunday (variable); Mother's Day, second Sunday in May; Memorial Day (half-staff until noon), May 30; Flag Day, June 14; Independence Day, July 4; Labor Day, first Monday in September; Constitution Day, September 17; Columbus Day, October 12; Navy Day, October 27; Veterans Day, November 11; Thanksgiving Day, fourth Thursday in November; Christmas Day, December 25; such other days as may be proclaimed by the President of the United States; the birthdays of States (dates of admission); and on State holidays.

(e) The flag should be displayed daily, weather permitting, on or near the main administration building of every public institution.

(f) The flag should be displayed in or near every polling place on election days.

(g) The flag should be displayed during school days in or near every schoolhouse.

(June 22, 1942, ch. 435, § 2, 56 Stat. 435; Dec. 22, 1942, ch. 806, § 2, 56 Stat. 1074.)

CODIFICATION

Veterans Day was substituted for Armistice Day, to conform to the provisions of act June 1, 1954, ch. 250, 68 Stat. 168. See section 87a of Title 5, Executive Departments and Government Officers and Employees.

AMENDMENTS

1942 — Par. (d) amended by act Dec. 22, 1942, which substituted "fourth Thursday in November" for "last Thursday in November."

FLAG HOUSE SQUARE, BALTIMORE, MARYLAND: DISPLAY OF FLAG; TIME

Act Mar. 26, 1954, ch. 109, 68 Stat. 35, provided:

"That notwithstanding any rule or custom pertaining to the display of the flag of the United States of America as set forth in the joint resolution entitled 'Joint resolution to codify and emphasize existing rules and customs pertaining to the display and use of the flag of the United States of America,' approved June 22, 1942, as amended [sections 171—178 of this title], authority is hereby conferred on the appropriate officer of the State of Maryland to permit the flying of the flag of the United States for twenty-four hours of each day in Flag House Square, Albemarle and Pratt Streets, Baltimore, Maryland.

"SEC. 2. Subject to the provisions of section 3 of the joint resolution of June 22, 1942, as amended [section 175 of this title], authority is also conferred on the appropriate officer of the State of Maryland to permit the flying of a replica of the flag of the United States which was in use during the War of 1812 for twenty-four hours of each day in Flag House Square, Albemarle and Pratt Streets, Baltimore, Maryland."

CROSS REFERENCES

National observances, display of flag on, see section 141 et seq. of this title.

§ 175. Same; position and manner of display.

The flag, when carried in a procession with another flag or flags, should be either on the marching right; that is, the flag's own right or, if there is a line of other flags, in front of the center of that line.

(a) The flag should not be displayed on a float in a parade except from a staff, or as provided in subsection (i) of this section.

(b) The flag should not be draped over the hood, top, sides, or back of a vehicle or of a railroad train or a boat. When the flag is displayed on a motorcar, the staff shall be fixed firmly to the chassis or clamped to the radiator cap.

(c) No other flag or pennant should be placed above or, if on the same level, to the right of the flag of the United States of America, except during church services conducted by naval chaplains at sea, when the church pennant may be flown above the flag during church services for the personnel of the Navy. No person shall display the flag of the United Nations or any other national or international flag equal, above, or in a position of superior prominence or honor to, or in place of, the flag of the United States at any place within the United States or any Territory or possession thereof: *Provided,* That nothing in this section shall make unlawful the continuance of the practice heretofore followed of displaying the flag of the United Nations in a position of superior prominence or honor, and other national flags in positions of equal prominence or honor, with that of the flag of the United States at the headquarters of the United Nations.

(d) The flag of the United States of America, when it is displayed with another flag against a wall from crossed staffs, should be on the right, the flag's own right, and its staff should be in front of the staff of the other flag.

(e) The flag of the United States of America should be at the center and at the highest point of the group when a number of flags of States or localities or pennants of societies are grouped and displayed from staffs.

(f) When flags of States, cities, or localities, or pennants of societies are flown on the same halyard with the flag of the United States, the latter should always be at the peak. When the flags are flown from adjacent staffs, the flag of the United States should be hoisted first and lowered last. No such flag or pennant may be placed above the flag of the United States or to the right of the flag of the United States.

(g) When flags of two or more nations are displayed, they are to be flown from separate staffs of the same height. The flags should be of approximately equal size. International usage forbids the display of the flag of one nation above that of another nation in time of peace.

(h) When the flag of the United States is displayed from a staff projecting horizontally or at an angle from the window sill, balcony, or front of a building, the union of the flag should be placed at the peak of the staff unless the flag is at half-staff. When the flag is suspended over a sidewalk from a rope extending from a house to a pole at the edge of the sidewalk, the flag should be hoisted out, union first, from the building.

(i) When the flag is displayed otherwise than by being flown from a staff, it should be displayed flat, whether indoors or out, or so suspended that its folds fall as free as though the flag were staffed.

(j) When the flag is displayed over the middle of the street, it should be suspended vertically with the union to the north in an east and west street or to the east in a north and south street.

(k) When used on a speaker's platform, the flag, if displayed flat, should be displayed above and behind the speaker. When displayed from a staff in a church or public auditorium, if it is displayed in the chancel of a church, or on the speaker's platform in a public auditorium,

the flag should occupy the position of honor and be placed at the clergyman's or speaker's right as he faces the congregation or audience. Any other flag so displayed in the chancel or on the platform should be placed at the clergyman's or speaker's left as he faces the congregation or audience. But when the flag is displayed from a staff in a church or public auditorium elsewhere than in the chancel or on the platform it shall be placed in the position of honor at the right of the congregation or audience as they face the chancel or platform. Any other flag so displayed should be placed on the left of the congregation or audience as they face the chancel or platform.

(l) The flag should form a distinctive feature of the ceremony of unveiling a statue or monument, but it should never be used as the covering for the statue or monument.

(m) The flag, when flown at half-staff, should be first hoisted to the peak for an instant and then lowered to the half-staff position. The flag should be again raised to the peak before it is lowered for the day. By "half-staff" is meant lowering the flag to one-half the distance between the top and bottom of the staff. Crepe streamers may be affixed to spearheads or flagstaffs in a parade only by order of the President of the United States.

(n) When the flag is used to cover a casket, it should be so placed that the union is at the head and over the left shoulder. The flag should not be lowered into the grave or allowed to touch the ground.

(June 22, 1942, ch. 435, § 3, 56 Stat. 379; Dec. 22, 1942, ch. 806, § 3, 56 Stat. 1075; July 9, 1953, ch. 183, 67 Stat. 142.)

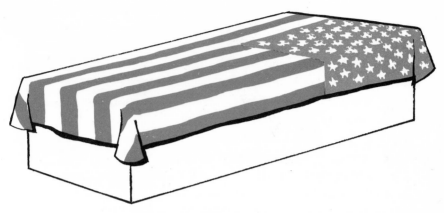

AMENDMENTS

1953 — Subsec. (c) amended by act July 9, 1953, which added second sentence.

1942 — Subsecs. (i) and (m) amended by act Dec. 22, 1942. Subsec. (i) was amended by adding "or so suspended that its folds fall as free as though the flag were staffed" and omitting provisions when displayed against a wall or in a window. Subsec. (m) was amended by substituting "lowering" for "hauling" in third sentence.

FLAG HOUSE SQUARE, BALTIMORE, MARYLAND; DISPLAY OF REPLICA OF FLAG USED IN WAR OF 1812; TIME

Display of replica of flag used in War of 1812 for twenty-four hours each day in Flag House Square, Baltimore, Maryland, as subject to this section, see note under section 174 of this title.

§ 176. Same; respect for flag.

No disrespect should be shown to the flag of the United States of America; the flag should not be dipped to any person or thing. Regimental colors, State flags, and organization or institutional flags are to be dipped as a mark of honor.

(a) The flag should never be displayed with the union down save as a signal of dire distress.

(b) The flag should never touch anything beneath it, such as the ground, the floor, water, or merchandise.

(c) The flag should never be carried flat or horizontally, but always aloft and free.

(d) The flag should never be used as drapery of any sort whatsoever, never festooned, drawn back, nor up, in folds, but always allowed to fall free. Bunting of blue, white, and red, always arranged with the blue above, the white in the middle, and the red below, should be used for covering a speaker's desk, draping the front of a platform, and for decoration in general.

(e) The flag should never be fastened, displayed, used, or stored in such a manner as will permit it to be easily torn, soiled, or damaged in any way.

(f) The flag should never be used as a covering for a ceiling.

(g) The flag should never have placed upon it, nor on any part of it, nor attached to it any mark, insignia, letter, word, figure, design, picture, or drawing of any nature.

(h) The flag should never be used as a receptacle for receiving, holding, carrying, or delivering anything.

(i) The flag should never be used for advertising purposes in any manner whatsoever. It should not be embroidered on such articles as cushions or handkerchiefs and the like, printed or otherwise impressed on paper napkins or boxes or anything that is designed for temporary use and discard; or used as any portion of a costume or athletic uniform. Advertising signs should not be fastened to a staff or halyard from which the flag is flown.

(j) The flag, when it is in such condition that it is no longer a fitting emblem for display, should be destroyed in a dignified way, preferably by burning.

(June 22, 1942, ch. 435, § 4, 56 Stat. 379; Dec. 22, 1942, ch. 806, § 4, 56 Stat. 1076.)

AMENDMENTS

1942 — Par. (g) amended by act Dec. 22, 1942, which inserted "any" before "part."

§ 177. Same; conduct during hoisting, lowering or passing of flag.

During the ceremony of hoisting or lowering the flag or when the flag is passing in a parade or in a review, all persons present should face the flag, stand at attention, and salute. Those present in uniform should render the military salute. When not in uniform, men should remove the headdress with the right hand holding it at the left shoulder, the hand being over the heart. Men without hats should salute in the same manner. Aliens should stand at attention. Women should salute by placing the right hand over the heart. The salute to the flag in the moving column should be rendered at the moment the flag passes.

(June 22, 1942, ch. 435, § 5, 56 Stat. 380; Dec. 22, 1942, ch. 806, § 5, 56 Stat. 1077.)

AMENDMENTS

1942 — Act Dec. 22, 1942, substituted "military salute," for "right-hand salute" in second sentence, "should salute in the same manner," for "merely stand at attention" in fourth sentence, and added fifth sentence.

CROSS REFERENCES

Alien as used in Immigration and Nationality Act defined, see section 1101 (a) (3) of Title 8, Aliens and Nationality.

§ 178. Same; modification of rules and customs by President.

Any rule or custom pertaining to the display of the flag of the United States of America, set forth in sections 171 — 178 of this title, may be altered, modified, or repealed, or additional rules with respect thereto may be prescribed, by the Commander in Chief of the Army and Navy of the United States, whenever he deems it to be appropriate or desirable; and any such alteration or additional rule shall be set forth in a proclamation.

(June 22, 1942, ch. 435, § 8, 56 Stat. 380; Dec. 22, 1942, ch. 806, § 8, 56 Stat. 1077.)

AMENDMENTS

1942 — Act Dec. 22, 1942, reenacted section without change.

Proc. No. 2605. THE FLAG OF THE UNITED STATES

Proc. No. 2605, Feb. 21, 1944, 9 F.R. 1957, 58 Stat. 1126, provided:

The flag of the United States of America is universally representative of the principles of the justice, liberty, and democracy enjoyed by the people of the United States; and

People all over the world recognize the flag of the United States as symbolic of the United States; and

The effective prosecution of the war requires a proper understanding by the people of other countries of the material assistance being given by the Government of the United States:

NOW, THEREFORE, by virtue of the power vested in me by the Constitution and laws of the United States, particularly by the Joint Resolution approved June 22, 1942, as amended by the Joint Resolution approved December 22, 1942 [sections 171—178 of this title], as President and Commander in Chief, it is hereby proclaimed as follows:

1. The use of the flag of the United States or any representation thereof, if approved by the Foreign Economic Administration, on labels, packages, cartons, cases, or other containers for articles or products of the United States intended for export as lend-lease aid, as relief and rehabilitation aid, or as emergency supplies for the Territories and possessions of the United States, or similar purposes, shall be considered a proper use of the flag of the United States and consistent with the honor and respect due to the flag.

2. If any article or product so labelled, packaged or otherwise bearing the flag of the United States or any representation thereof, as provided for in section 1, should, by force of circumstances, be diverted to the ordinary channels of domestic trade, no person shall be considered as violating the rules and customs pertaining to the display of the flag of the United States, as set forth in the Joint Resolution approved June 22, 1942, as amended by the Joint Resolution approved December 22, 1942 (U. S. C., Supp. II, title 36, secs. 171—178) [sections 171—178 of this title], for possessing, transporting, displaying, selling or otherwise transferring any such article or product solely because the label, package, carton, case, or other container bears the flag of the United States or any representation thereof.

INSTRUCTIONS FOR FLYING FLAG AT HALF-STAFF
ISSUED BY PRESIDENT EISENHOWER

Apparently, no definite instructions for flying the flag at half-staff were established in the early years of our country's history. As a result, many conflicting regulations existed. Accordingly, early in 1954, President Eisenhower issued instructions stating when, and for what length of time, the flag of the United States should fly at half-staff.

The proclamation provides for flying the flag at half-staff:

For thirty days from the day of death in the case of the President or a former President.

For ten days in the case of the death of the Vice President, the Chief Justice or a retired Chief Justice, or the Speaker of the House of Representatives.

From the day of death until interment for an Associate Justice of the Supreme Court, a member of the Cabinet, a former Vice President, the Secretaries of the Army, Navy and Air Force, a United States Senator, a member of the House, a territorial delegate, the Resident Commissioner from the Commonwealth of Puerto Rico, or the Governor of a state or territory.

In the event of the death of other officials, former officials or foreign dignitaries, the flag would be displayed at half-staff, in accordance with such orders or instructions as might be issued by or at the direction of the President, or "in accordance with recognized customs or practices not inconsistent with law."

The President's proclamation also stated that the heads of departments and agencies of the Federal Government might direct that the flag be flown at half-staff on occasions other than those specified which they consider proper.

Interesting Flag Information

As a gesture of patriotism and in cooperation with the American Legion, various dry cleaners throughout the United States will clean the flag free of charge during the period from June 1 to 12, provided the owner agrees to fly the flag on Flag Day, June 14.

No flag should be flown above the Stars and Stripes except in the following situations: (1) the church pennant during divine services conducted at sea by naval chaplains; (2) the United Nations flag at the United Nations Headquarters. (See U.S. Code, Sec. 175, par. c.)

Displaying the flag inverted, that is, with the union down is a signal of dire distress. (See U.S. Code, Sec. 176, par. a.)

"Striking the Colors" means to lower the flag to half-staff (one-half the distance between the top and bottom of the staff). It indicates submission or surrender.

Flying the flag at half-mast is a symbol of mourning.

Should the death of a serviceman or woman occur during a period of service, the flag is provided by the Service.

The flag for the burial service of an honorably discharged veteran is furnished by the Veterans Administration, Washington, D.C. It may be obtained from the nearest post office upon the presentation of proper proof of honorable discharge. The flag must be presented to the next of kin at the appropriate moment in the burial service. Should there be no relative present, or one cannot be located, the flag must be returned to the Veterans Administration.

ORIGIN OF THE TERM "OLD GLORY"

Old Glory is a popular name for the flag of the United States. Accounts of its origin vary. The following explanation appears credible.

William Driver (1810-1886), a sea captain of Salem, Massachusetts, was presented with a flag by a group of Salem citizens on the occasion of his embarkation on a round-the-world voyage in 1831. As the flag was hoisted and unfurled, the captain shouted, "I'll call her Old Glory, boys, Old Glory!"

He kept the flag and, upon his retirement, brought it with him to Nashville, Tennessee, where it sometimes was flown before his house. The flag was put away at the beginning of the Civil War and it was brought out only after General William Nelson's wing of the Union Army took Nashville on February 27, 1862.

The original Old Glory remained with Captain Driver's descendants until 1922, when it was placed on display in the Smithsonian Institute at Washington, D.C.

Glossary

A number of words are used in special senses to describe flags and parts of flags. A selection of these terms is given here:

BADGE: An emblem or other device displayed on a flag, generally in the *fly*.

BANNER: Originally a large medieval flag, rectangular in shape and usually carried in battle. Today the word is synonymous with *flag*.

CANTON: The four quarters of a flag are named *cantons*, but this word is applied particularly to the upper canton in the hoist, that is, the upper left hand corner of the flag; the canton is sometimes also called the *union*.

COLOR: Specifically, a flag carried by an infantry or other dismounted military unit; more generally, any flag, as in the phrase, *national colors*.

COMMAND FLAG: A flag flown by naval officers of high rank from their flagships; also, similar flags used by military and air force officers.

DIPPING: Practice, formerly followed, of merchant vessels lowering their ensigns in salute on meeting a naval vessel. The practice was also, on occasion, observed between warships.

ESCUTCHEON: The surface upon which armorial emblems are exhibited.

☆ 87

FIELD: The surface of a flag on which the *canton, badges,* and other devices and designs are placed.

FLY: The portion of a flag farthest from the *hoist.*

GUIDON: A small military flag, usually carried by small units as a distinguishing device.

HOIST: The portion of a flag nearest the flagstaff.

HOUSE FLAG: A small flag used by shipping lines and, similarly, any such flag used by a commercial or other organization.

JACK: A flag, smaller than the *ensign,* flown at the bow by warships when at anchor or dressed with flags for a special event. Occasionally, it is also flown by other vessels.

MERCHANT FLAG: A flag flown by a commercial or other private vessel; sometimes the same as the *national flag,* sometimes different from it.

NATIONAL COLOR: A term designating the United States Flag carried by dismounted or unmounted units.

NATIONAL ENSIGN: A term designating the United States Flag flown by airships, ships and boats.

NATIONAL FLAG: A flag representing a country; its use is sometimes restricted to the Government, but more often extended to the citizens in general. The term, when applied specifically to the United States Flag, refers to that flag in general without regard to a particular size or manner of display.

NATIONAL STANDARD: A term designating the United States Flag carried by mounted, mechanized and motorized units.

PENNANT or PENDANT: A narrow flag which tapers gently toward the *fly.* Warships frequently fly *masthead pennants.*

STANDARD: Originally, a medieval flag of a long tapering shape; now used to denote flags carried by cavalry or other mounted troops.

SWALLOW-TAILED FLAGS: A flag whose *fly* is divided by one or two slits into two or three distinct tails. A number of modern Scandinavian flags are swallow-tailed.

UNION: A design, signifying union, used on a national emblem. It is the honor point of the flag. On the United States Flag, it is the blue field containing the group of white stars.

State Flags

ALABAMA
December 14, 1819

ALASKA
January 3, 1959

ARIZONA
February 19, 1912

ARKANSAS
June 15, 1836

CALIFORNIA
September 9, 1850

COLORADO
August 1, 1876

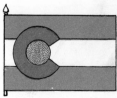

☆ 89

IDAHO
July 3, 1890

CONNECTICUT
January 9, 1788

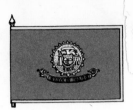

ILLINOIS
December 3, 1818

DELAWARE
December 7, 1787

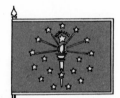

INDIANA
December 11, 1816

FLORIDA
March 3, 1845

IOWA
December 28, 1846

GEORGIA
January 2, 1788

KANSAS
January 29, 1861
Unofficial

HAWAII
August 21, 1959

KENTUCKY
June 1, 1792
Unofficial

LOUISIANA
April 30, 1812

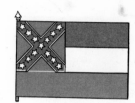

MISSISSIPPI
December 10, 1817

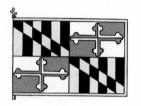

MAINE
March 15, 1820

MISSOURI
August 10, 1821

MARYLAND
April 28, 1788

MONTANA
November 8, 1889

MASSACHUSETTS
February 6, 1788

NEBRASKA
March 1, 1867

MICHIGAN
January 26, 1837

NEVADA
October 31, 1864

MINNESOTA
May 11, 1858

 91

NORTH DAKOTA
November 2, 1889

NEW HAMPSHIRE
June 21, 1788

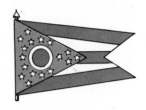

OHIO
February 19, 1803

NEW JERSEY
December 18, 1787

OKLAHOMA
November 16, 1907

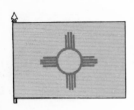

NEW MEXICO
January 6, 1912

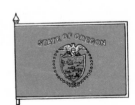

OREGON
February 14, 1859

NEW YORK
July 26, 1788

PENNSYLVANIA
December 12, 1787

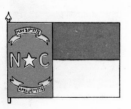

NORTH CAROLINA
November 21, 1789

RHODE ISLAND
May 29, 1790

SOUTH CAROLINA
May 23, 1788

VIRGINIA
June 26, 1788

SOUTH DAKOTA
November 2, 1889

WASHINGTON
November 11, 1889

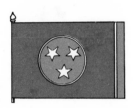

TENNESSEE
June 1, 1796

WEST VIRGINIA
June 20, 1863

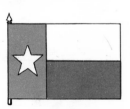

TEXAS
December 29, 1845

WISCONSIN
May 29, 1848

UTAH
January 4, 1896

WYOMING
July 11, 1890

VERMONT
March 4, 1791